AF217936

Sally

Lehrwerk für den
Englischunterricht ab Klasse 3

Pupil's Book 4

Erarbeitet von
Martina Bredenbröcker
Jasmin Brune
Daniela Elsner
Barbara Gleich
Stefanie Gleixner-Weyrauch
Simone Gutwerk
Marion Lugauer
Sabine Schwarz

Unter Beratung von
Jane Brockmann-Fairchild

Illustriert von
Barbara Jung, Wilfried Poll,
Anja Boretzki, Andreas Fischer, Renate Möller,
Thilo Pustlauk, Gisela Vogel

Oldenbourg Schulbuchverlag, München

Inhalt

 pupil's CD / teacher's CD

 teacher's CD only

Sally's task

extra

 Work with a partner.

Work in groups.

 Write.

 Draw.

 Speak.

Rap: Welcome back to school!

Susan

Step to the left, step to the right.

Raise your and feel alright.

Turn around and say, "That's cool!"

Welcome back to school!

Tim

Eric

Sit on your , write in the air.

Let's have fun with English.

Dance to the beat and say, "That's cool!"

Welcome back to school!

Emily

Phil

Around the classroom you must look.

Put your on the .

Turn around and say, "That's cool!"

Welcome back to school!

Liz

1  **Listen and sing.**

2  **Act out the rap.**

Let's rap!

Let's play a board game!

1 **Play in groups (2–5).**
Roll the dice. Take turns.

Red number:
Do what it says or answer
the question.
If you can't, miss a turn.

The winner is the first
to reach finish.

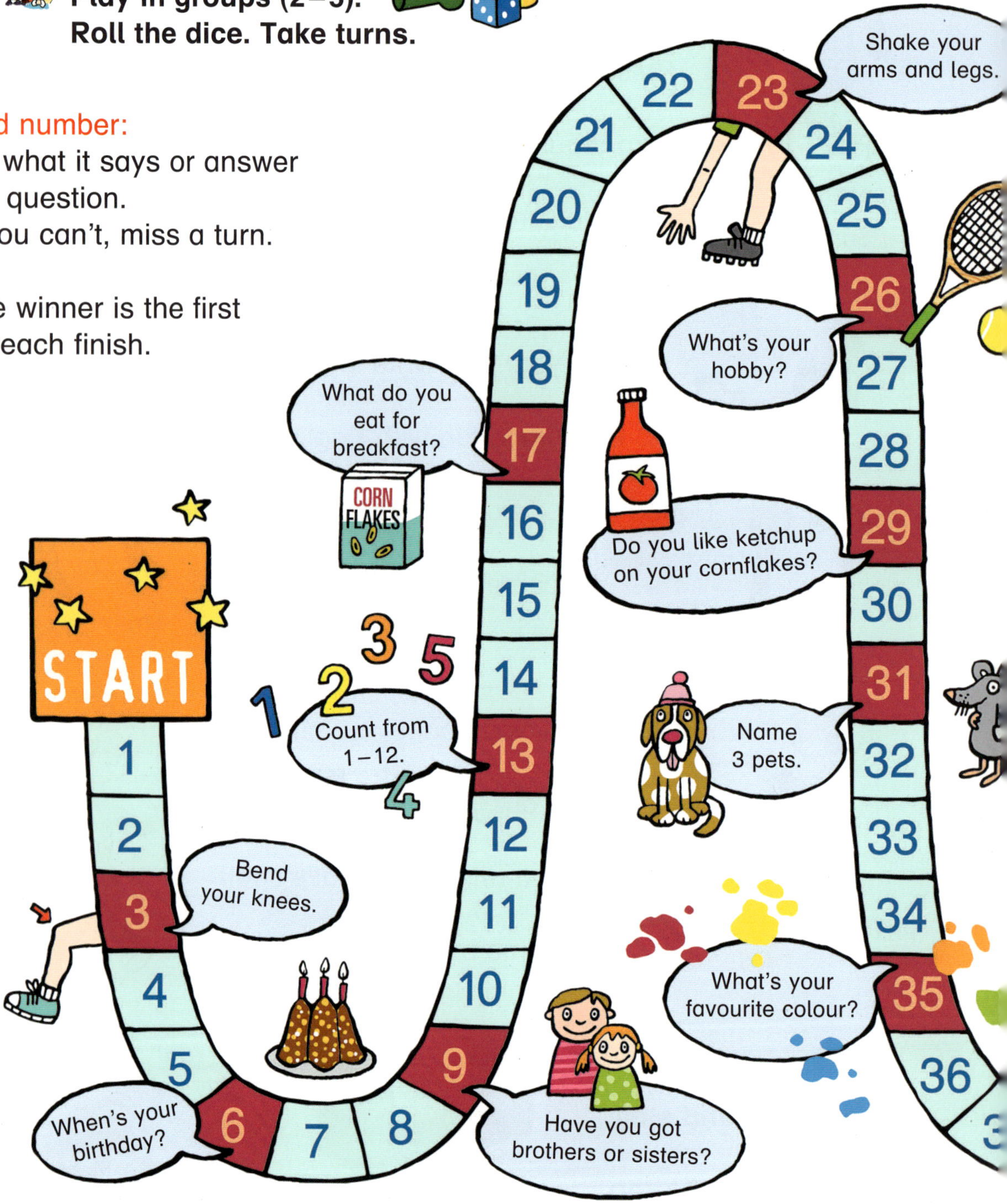

START

Bend
your knees.

When's your
birthday?

Count from
1–12.

What do you
eat for
breakfast?

CORN
FLAKES

Have you got
brothers or sisters?

What's your
favourite colour?

Name
3 pets.

Do you like ketchup
on your cornflakes?

What's your
hobby?

Shake your
arms and legs.

1 2 3 4 5 6 7 8 9 10 11 12 13 14 15 16 17 18 19 20 21 22 23 24 25 26 27 28 29 30 31 32 33 34 35 36

2 Do the English rally.

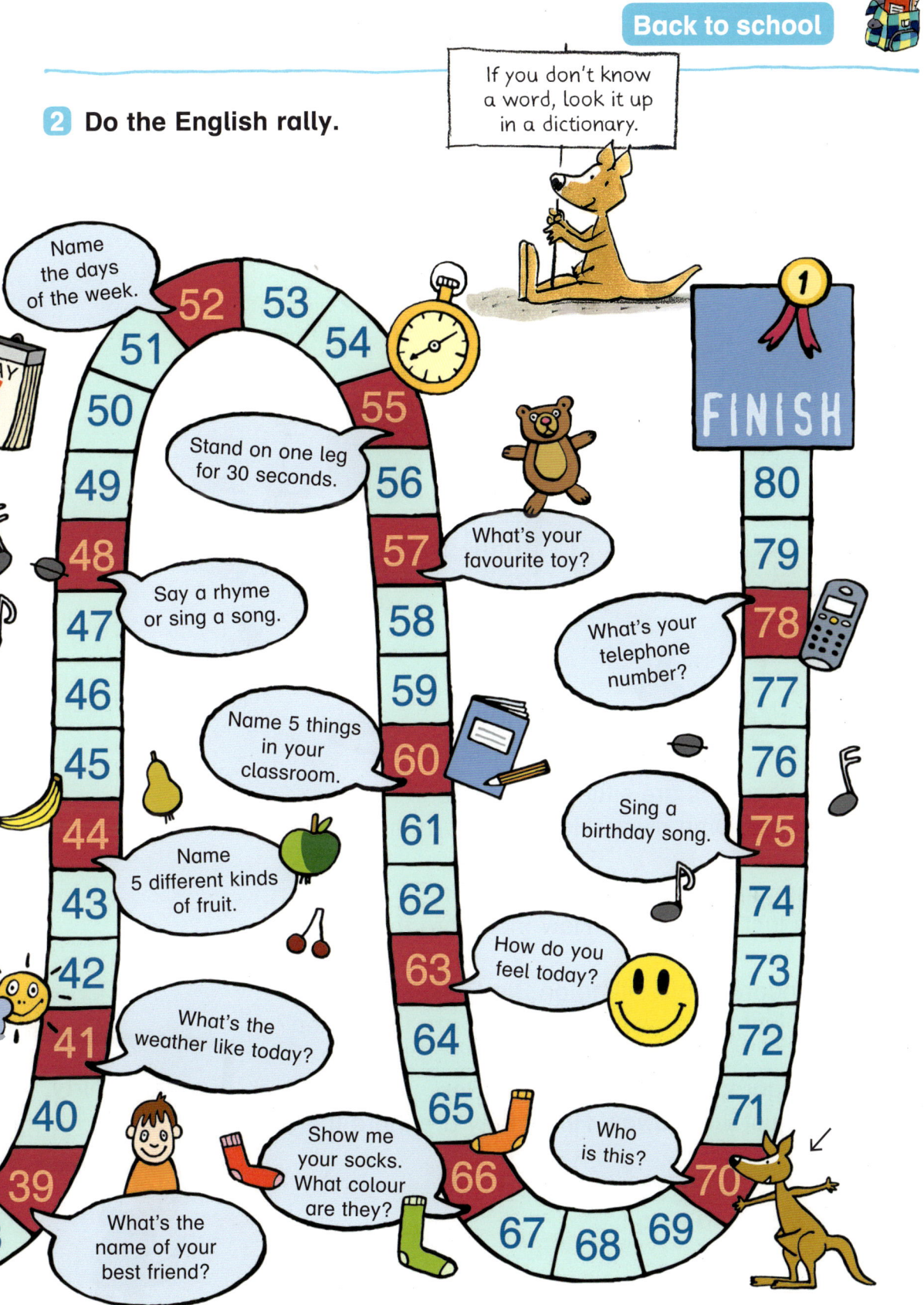

If you don't know a word, look it up in a dictionary.

Name the days of the week.

Stand on one leg for 30 seconds.

Say a rhyme or sing a song.

What's your favourite toy?

What's your telephone number?

Name 5 things in your classroom.

Sing a birthday song.

Name 5 different kinds of fruit.

How do you feel today?

What's the weather like today?

Show me your socks. What colour are they?

Who is this?

What's the name of your best friend?

FINISH

100 little kangaroos are sitting on Big Ben

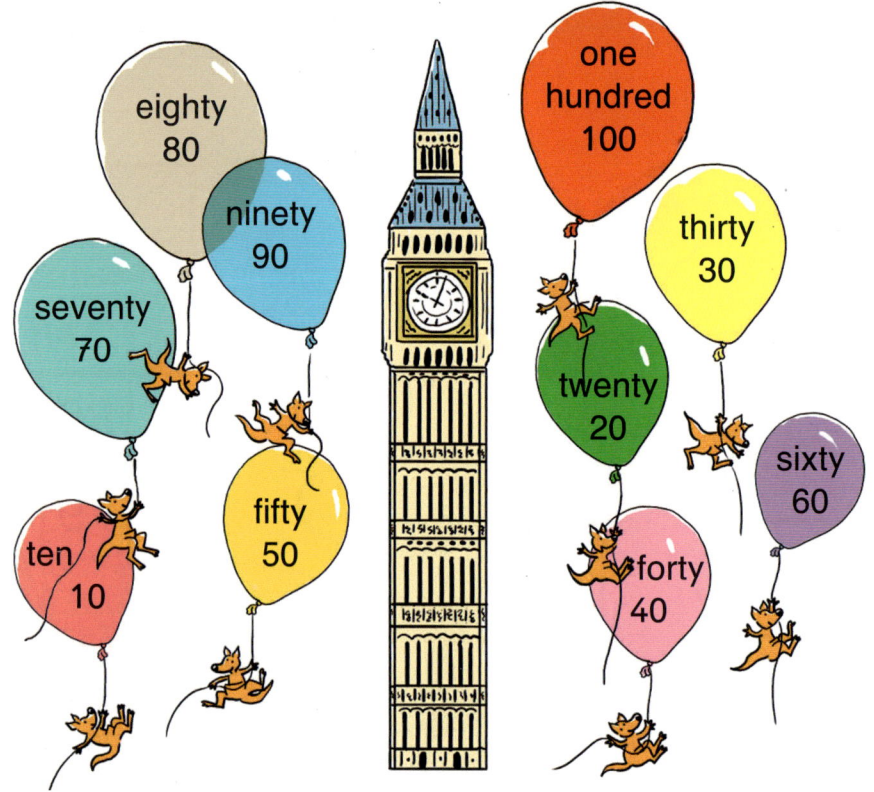

100 little kangaroos are sitting on Big Ben.
10 of them just jump away. How many are there then?

90 little kangaroos are sitting on Big Ben.
10 of them just jump away. How many are there then?

80 little kangaroos are sitting on Big Ben.
10 of them just jump away. How many are there then?

70 little kangaroos are sitting on Big Ben.
10 of them just jump away. How many are there then?
…

1 🔘 **Listen and sing.**

2 **Sing the song faster and faster.**

twen**ty**, thir**ty**, for**ty**, …

Gavin the ghost

Gavin is angry. He has got the hiccups …

Hic! Hic!

… in the kitchen …

Hic! Hic!

Can you stop my hiccups?

Drink a glass of water. Don't breathe.

Hic! Hic!

… in the living room …

Stand on your head. Sing a song.

Head and shoulders, …

Hic! Hic!

… in the bathroom …

Hold your nose. Count from 20 to 30.

Hic!

… in the bedroom …

Let's play hide-and-seek!

Hic!

20, 21, 22, 23, …

Gavin looks for his family.

Hic! Hic!

Gavin sits on the stairs.

Boo!

Aargh!

Hooray! My hiccups are gone!

Hic!

1 🔘 **Listen and read.**

2 👨‍👩‍👧 **Act out the story.**

At the hotel

Perfect holiday
in a Scottish castle.

Nice rooms …
Only 99 pounds a week!
Great offer …

The bed is too small.

The chair is too big.

… for dwarfs and giants!

1 Look at the hotel. What's wrong?
Tell your partner.

2 Design your own special hotel.

Let's make Sally's sandwich!

You need:
bread
ketchup
mustard
a tomato
a cucumber
ham
cheese
lettuce

Take a slice of bread.
Put it on a plate.

Spread ketchup and mustard on it.

Cut the tomato and the cucumber.
Put them on the bread.

Put some ham, cheese and lettuce on it.

Put another slice of bread on top.

Cut the sandwich in half.
Sally's sandwich is ready to eat!

1 **Look and read.**

2 **Make your own sandwich:**
What do you want to put on your sandwich? Make a shopping list in your group. Talk about who wants to bring the bread, ham, …

Let's have lunch

In the restaurant

diner

hot dog stand

fish and chips shop

salad bar

Can I help you?

I'd like ...

1 Look and read.

2 Listen to the text.
What do Emily and Phil order?

3 Where do you have lunch?
Act out the scene.

Hobbies

riding a horse	riding a bike	playing the guitar
reading books	ice skating	playing the piano	snowboarding
	playing football	swimming

I **like** swimming.

He/She **likes** swimming.

1 Look at the children.
What are their hobbies?
Tim's hobby is … / Tim likes …

2 What's your hobby?
Show your photos and tell your class:
My hobby is … / I like …

The interview

1  **Ask your partner.**

Can you …?

Yes, I can.

No, I can't.

Can you
- play football
- sing a song
- play the guitar
- ride a skateboard
- inline skate

?

2  **Listen to the interview with Dirk Nowitzki.**

Dirk Nowitzki likes playing basketball.

3 **Do your own interview.**

I can sing.
I like sing**ing**.

Emily's day

At 8 o'clock I get up and have breakfast.

School begins at 9 o'clock.

At half past 12 I have lunch.

At 3 o'clock I go home.

At quarter to 4 I do my homework.

At 5 o'clock I call my friends and we play football.

At half past 6 I have dinner.

At 8 o'clock I read a book or watch TV.

At quarter past 9 I go to bed. Good night!

1 Listen, look and read.

2 **What about your day? Tell your partner:**
In the morning …
In the afternoon …
In the evening / At night …

⭐ **And what do you do on a Sunday?**

> MY SUNDAY
> On Sunday, I get up at …

At the same time

Somewhere in the world school starts.
At the same time …

... a little cat
spills a glass of lemonade …

... a shark
looks for some food
in the ocean …

... a baby eats
some chocolate
ice cream ...

... a skateboard
rolls down a hill …

... a father forgets
about his pancake ...

... a mouse kisses
a horse ...

... somewhere in the world school is over.

1 **Look and read.**

2 **What else happens at the same time?
Talk to your class.**

3 **Make your own storybook.
Use a dictionary.**

> I eat.
> He/She/It eat**s**.

In the supermarket

Special offer!

chocolate bars

bread   rolls

biscuits   jam

coffee   tea

drinks

lemonade

juice

water

Pay here!

SUPER MARKET

milk

cheese

butter   eggs

honey

pineapples

apples

bananas

lemons

oranges

cherries

spinach

pears

1 🔘 **Listen and point.**

2 ✏️ **Make your own shopping list.**

3 👦👧 **Talk to your partner.**

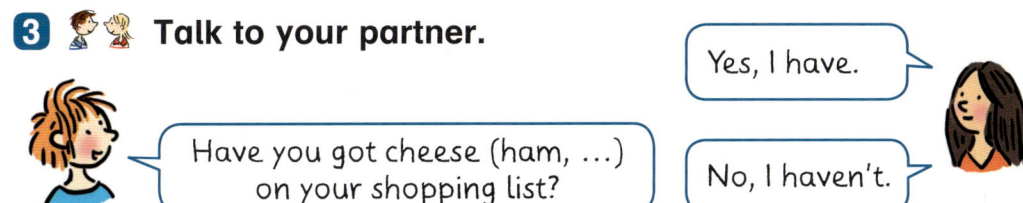

Have you got cheese (ham, …) on your shopping list?

Yes, I have.

No, I haven't.

Something good

1 Listen to the story and point to the pictures.

2 Can you tell the story?

3 What can you buy in a supermarket?

Tyya went shopping with her father.

 "My gets   ."

Tyya put 100 boxes of into her cart.

 "Daddy, look! Good food!"

 "Oh, no! Put it all back!"

Tyya put back the 100 boxes of . She put 300 into her cart.

 "Daddy, look! Good food!"

 "Oh, no! Put it all back! Don't move."

Tyya didn't move. A lady came by and looked at Tyya.
The lady put a price tag on Tyya's .
She picked Tyya up and put her
on the shelf with all the other dolls.

A man came along and looked at Tyya.

 "I'm going to get that for my son."

 "STOP!"

Then Tyya's father came along.

 "Tyya? Tyya? Where are you? What are you doing on that shelf?"

He gave Tyya a big kiss. Then they went to pay.

 "Hey, Mister. You have to pay for her."

 "This is my kid. I won't pay."

"Yes!"

"NO!"

Daddy paid the man. Tyya gave her father a big kiss.

"Daddy, you finally bought something good."

4   **Read the text. Practise in your group.**

Jack and the beanstalk

The illustrated story panels contain:

We must sell the cow.

Fee, fi, foe, fum! I smell the blood of an Englishman.

Here are five magic beans for your cow.

I must climb it.

Now we can buy a new cow!

A castle, a kitchen and an apple pie. Yummy!

 **1** Listen, look and point.

 **2** Act out the story.

This giant is really tall and bad!

CD 1.27

Let's act it out!

Reading and learning the story

Painting the background

Making the music

Telling the story with shadow puppets

Practising the story

Performing the story

Flying to London

1 **Look and read.**

KANGAROO AIRLINE

NAME: SALLY MACJUMP

FLIGHT NUMBER: KA 77

FLIGHT: SYDNEY – LONDON

DATE: 8 AUGUST

GATE: A1

BOARDING TIME: 12:30

NAME: SALLY MACJUMP

SEAT NUMBER: B 15

The red double-decker bus is famous in London.

The traditional London taxi is black. You drive on the left-hand side of the road.

The underground in London is one of the oldest in the world.

There are lots of ferries on the River Thames.

2 **Look at the photos and read.**

 Compare to other cities. Where do you live? What can you see in your town? Talk to your partner.

Detective Brighthead

1 Listen to the story and look at the pictures.

2 What forms of transport does Mr Brighthead take?
He takes the …

The clever tortoise

 Listen, look and read.

The five-minute zoo game

Play with a partner.

Play for five minutes.

Roll the dice.

Take turns.

The winner is the player who has got the most points.

Start

Move in any direction.

Animal picture:
Name the animal = 1 point.
Name the animal and describe it = 2 points.

Snack stop: You must pay. Miss a turn.

Crocodile: Bad luck! You lose 1 point.

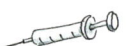

At the doctor's

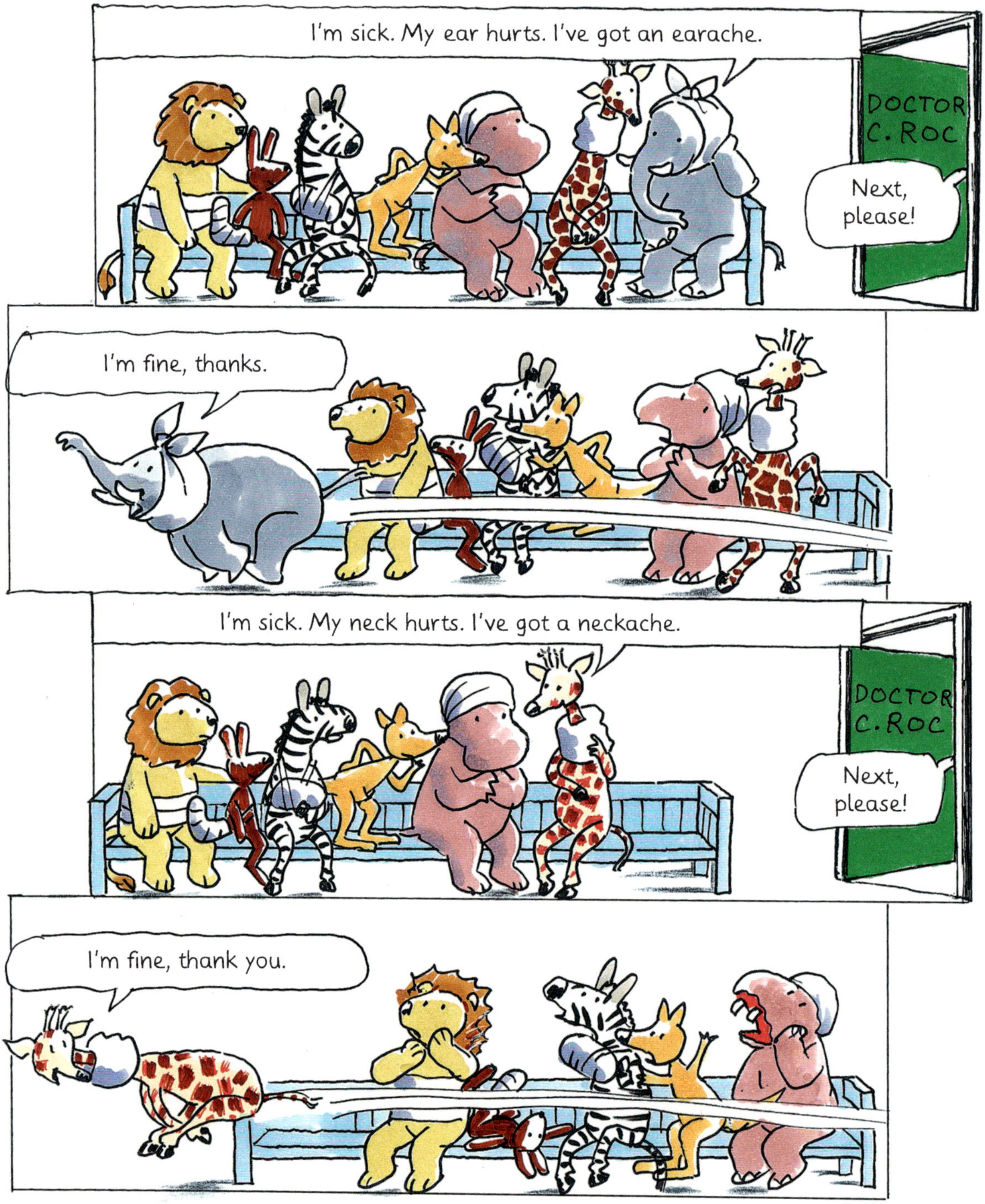

I'm sick. My head hurts. I've got a headache.

DOCTOR C. ROC

Next, please!

I'm fine, thanks.

I'm sick. My back hurts. I've got a backache.

DOCTOR C. ROC

Next, please!

I'm fine, thank you.

1 **Look and read.**

2 **Why do the animals run away? Guess.**

3 **Act out the story.**

The inline skating accident

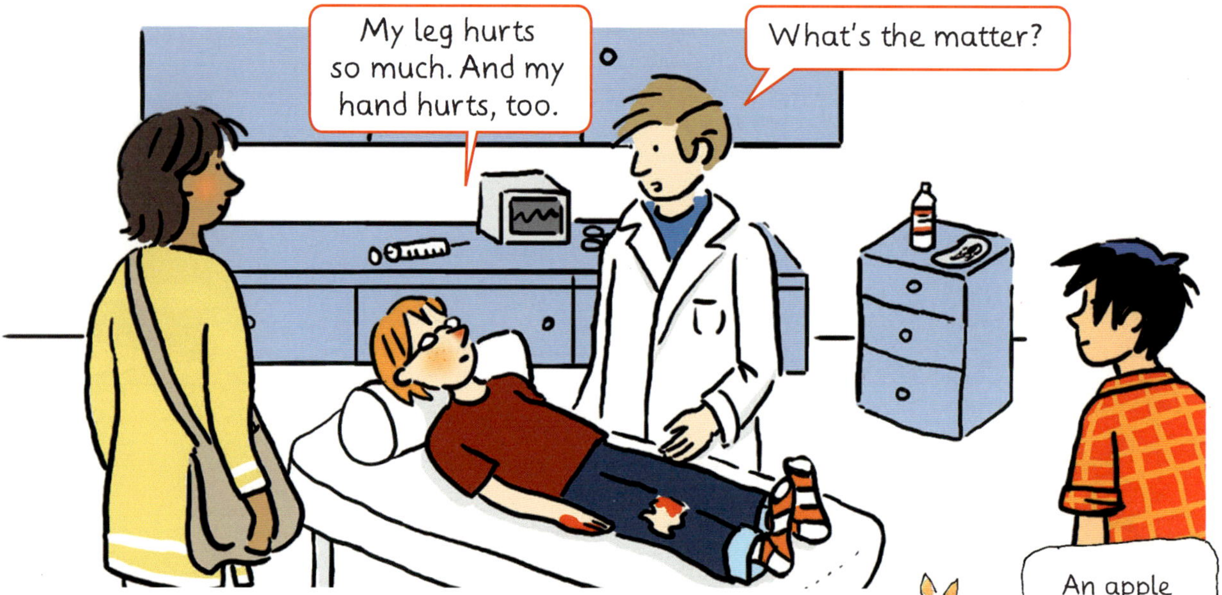

1 💬 **Look and speak.**

2 ✏️ **Look at the people in the waiting room.**
   What's the matter?
   Write a sentence about each patient.
   The boy has got a headache …

headache   neckache
earache   backache

First aid

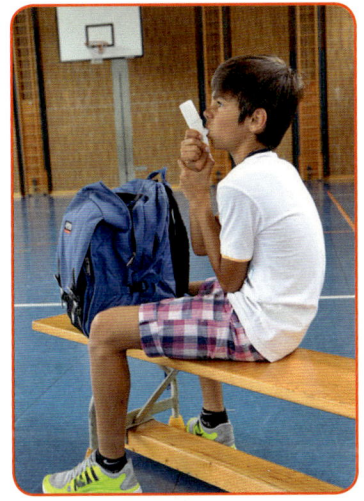
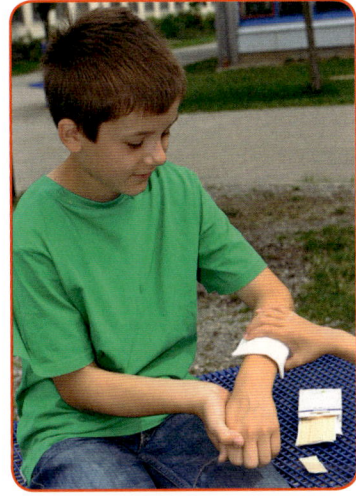

Here is what you can do

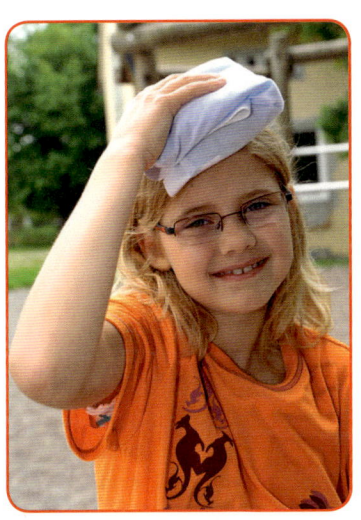

Sit down.
Get your medicine.
Cool it.
Get a plaster
or a bandage.
Put pressure
on the wound.
Call 112.

I'll help you!

1  **Listen and point.**

2 **What can you do? Tell your partner.**

3 **Make a first-aid book.**

 **Going to Scotland**

Sally and the Loch Ness Monster

A photo of the Loch Ness Monster!

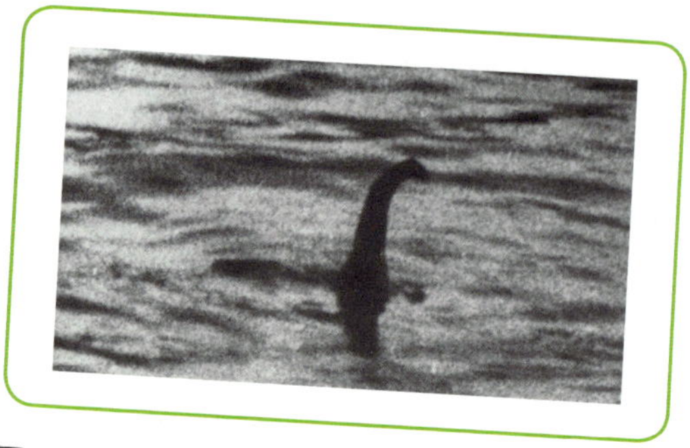

Welcome!

Hello!

Where is Nessie?

Where is Nessie?

Goodbye, Uncle!

Robert, Sally, look at this photo!

There's Nessie in the lake!

1 Listen, look and point.

2 Read and tell the story.

3 Draw your own Nessie. Describe her to your class.

A holiday trip to Scotland

> I want to go to a castle.

> I want to see the Highland Mountains and go fishing.

> I want to visit the Highland Games.

> I want to go to the sea.

> And we all want to see Nessie!

1 💬 **Look and speak:**
Mr Brown wants to see …

2 🐕 **Plan your own holiday trip to Scotland.**
Find out about Scotland on the Internet.

Scottish dance

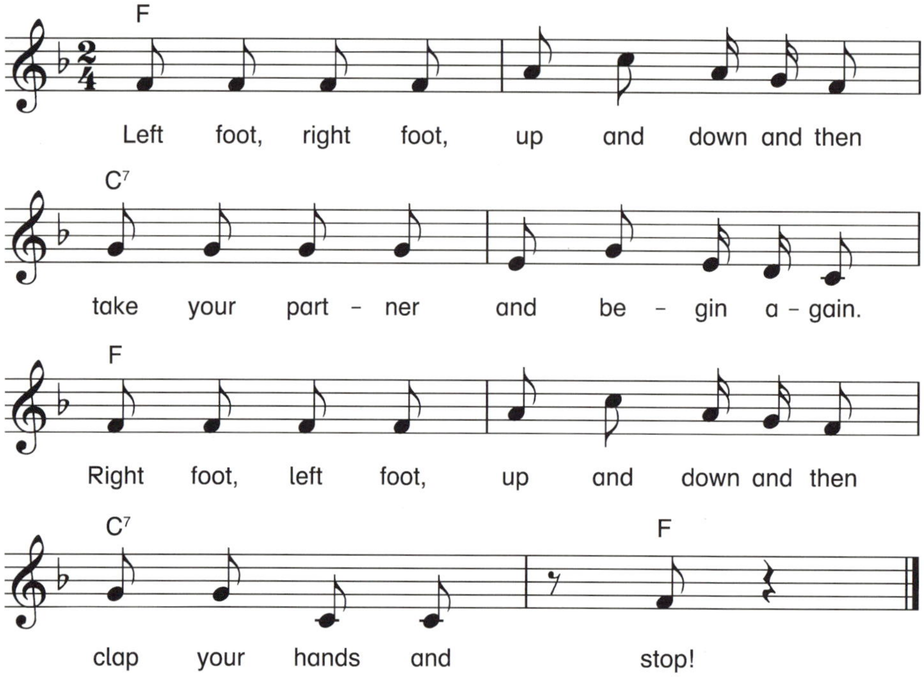

F

Left foot, right foot, up and down and then

C⁷

take your part – ner and be – gin a – gain.

F

Right foot, left foot, up and down and then

C⁷   **F**

clap your hands and stop!

Today I'm wearing my kilt.

1 🔘 **Listen, sing and dance.**

2 **Do the rallies.**

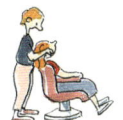
What do you want to be?

shop assistant

hairdresser

teacher

football player

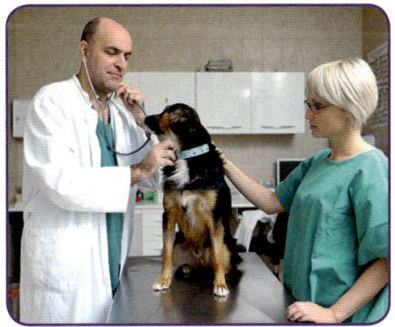

vet

doctor

policewoman

1  **Listen and point.**

2 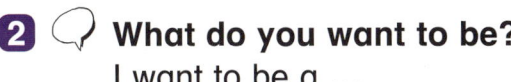 **What do you want to be?**
I want to be a …

I want to be a superstar!

My jobs

I have to help in the garden.

I have to tidy my room.

I have to do
my homework.

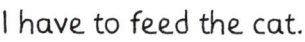

I have to feed the cat.

I have to make my bed.

I have to walk the dog.

I have to help
in the kitchen.

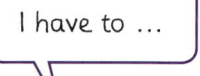

I have to …

1 **Look and read.**

2  **What do you have to do?**
I have to …

3 **Do a job survey in your class.**

A rainbow of friends

Some friends are funny.

Some friends are stars.

Some friends wear clothing that's different than ours.

But all friends are special.

We all have our interests.

We all have our strengths and weaknesses too.

If we work hand in hand, all jobs can be done.

If we play as a team, we've already won.

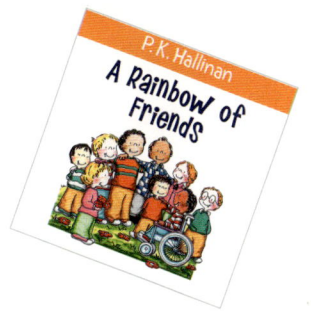

P.K. Hallinan
A Rainbow of Friends

1 Read the story and tell.

2 What's special about your friends? Tell.

We all live in the same world

Hola!

Juanita

Bonjour!

Jacqueline

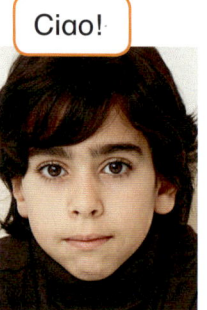

Ciao!

Paolo

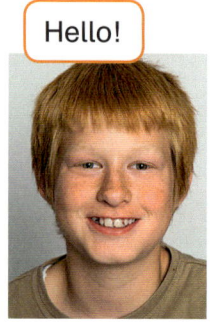

Hello!

Thomas

Hallo!

Maria

Merhaba!

Güler

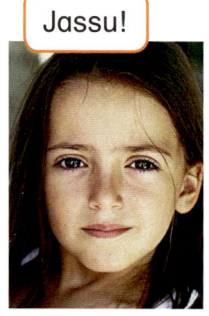

Jassu!

Dimitra

Priwjet!

Sergej

I'm from …	I speak …
England	English
France	French
Germany	German
Greece	Greek
Italy	Italian
Russia	Russian
Spain	Spanish
Turkey	Turkish

But we all laugh in the same language.
We all like to sing and play.
We all live in the same world,
no matter where we're from.

1 **Listen and sing.**

2 **Where are you from? What language(s) do you speak?**

⭐ **What's the word for** Hello **in different languages?
Make a list.**

Guy Fawkes Day – Bonfire Night

Penny for the guy!

5th November
Guy Fawkes Day

fireworks at night

bonfire at night

Do you know why people celebrate Guy Fawkes Day?

1 💬 **Look at the pictures. Read the text.**

2 💿 **Listen to the story about Guy Fawkes.**

⭐ **Do you know other festivals with fireworks or bonfires?**

Thanksgiving today

Mum gets up at 6 o'clock in the morning.
She puts the turkey into the oven.
The turkey takes five hours to cook.

At 12 o'clock my family comes to our house. We have our Thanksgiving dinner: turkey with potatoes, carrots, corncobs and pumpkin pie.

In the afternoon we go to the Thanksgiving parade.

In the evening we watch the football match on TV.

1  **Listen to the story of Carol's Thanksgiving.**

2 **Look at the photos and read.**

A turkey is a funny bird, his head goes wobble, wobble. And he knows just one word: "Gobble, gobble, gobble!"

CD 2.23

A story about the first Thanksgiving

The first Thanksgiving

1 💿 **Listen to the story about the first Thanksgiving.**

2 💬 **Look at the picture. What can you see?**

> pumpkin   corncobs   potatoes   beans   tomatoes
> turkey   Indians   settlers   fishing

3 💬 **What do you know about the American Indians?**

CD 2.24   thirty-nine **39**

Come to the USA!

A cowboy in Texas shows how he works.

The Mississippi is a very long river.
You can take a ride on a steamboat.

The Grand Canyon National Park is in
Arizona. The views are great!

The Statue of Liberty is in New York.

The President of the USA lives in the
White House in Washington, D.C.

In San Francisco, California, cable cars
go up and down the roads.

1 **Look at the photos.**

2 ○ **What do you know about the USA?**

3 **Make a poster, a collage or a report about the USA.**
   Present it to your class.

Father Christmas in Australia

1 🔘 **Listen and point.**

2 **Read.**

3 👧 **Act out the story.**

The five days of Christmas

On the first day of Christmas
my true love sent to me
a  in a gum tree.

On the second day of Christmas
my true love sent to me

two small

and a in a gum tree.

kookaburra

koala

On the third day of Christmas
my true love sent to me

three ,

two small …

cockatoo

On the fourth day of Christmas
my true love sent to me

four ,

three …

crocodile

On the fifth day of Christmas
my true love sent to me

five ,

four …

kangaroo

1  **Look at the photos. Listen and sing.**

2 ✎ **Write word cards for a Christmas bingo.**
sleigh, reindeer, stocking, present, star,
Christmas tree, winter, cold, snowy…

Let's go to Australia!

Sydney is the biggest city.

A road train is a very long truck.

Ayers Rock is a big flat rock.

At the Great Barrier Reef you can see coral and coloured fish.

An Australian Aborigine is playing the didgeridoo.

1 Look at the photos.

2 Listen and point.

3 Read the text. Find the correct photo.

⭐ Look and draw your own traffic sign.

Next 92 km

G'day!

Let's make an Easter bunny mosaic card!

You need:
coloured eggshells
cardboard
a pencil
glue
scissors

Break the eggshells
into small pieces.

Draw your Easter bunny
on the cardboard. Cut it out.

Glue the eggshells on your
Easter bunny.

Glue your Easter bunny
onto the cardboard. Write an
Easter greeting on your card.

1  **Look and read. Make your own Easter card.
Write "Happy Easter!" on your card.**

2 Can you say "Happy Easter!" in other languages?

 ## Back to school
Zurück in der Schule

eleven   elf
twelve   zwölf
thirteen   dreizehn
fourteen   vierzehn
fifteen   fünfzehn
sixteen   sechzehn
seventeen   siebzehn
eighteen   achtzehn
nineteen   neunzehn
twenty   zwanzig
thirty   dreißig
forty   vierzig
fifty   fünfzig
sixty   sechzig
seventy   siebzig
eighty   achtzig
ninety   neunzig
a/one hundred   hundert

clock   Uhr
hand   (Uhr-)Zeiger
(to) set   stellen

What time is it?   Wie spät ist es?

It's 1 (2, 3 ...) o'clock.
Es ist 1 (2, 3 ...) Uhr.

It's quarter past 1 (2, 3 ...).
Es ist viertel nach 1 (2, 3 ...).

It's half past 1 (2, 3...).
Es ist halb 2 (3, 4 ...).

It's quarter to 2 (3, 4 ...).
Es ist viertel vor 2 (3, 4 ...).

 ## At home   Zu Hause

attic   Speicher
bathroom   Badezimmer
bedroom   Schlafzimmer
castle   Schloss, Burg
cellar   Keller
garden   Garten
hiccups   Schluckauf
kitchen   Küche
living room   Wohnzimmer
stairs   Treppen
toilet   Toilette, WC

bed   Bett
chair   Stuhl
furniture   Möbel
just right   genau richtig
lamp   Lampe
shelves   Regal
sofa   Sofa
table   Tisch
too big   zu groß
too small   zu klein
wardrobe   Schrank

Where is ...? – He/She/It is in the ...
Wo ist ...? – Er/Sie/Es ist im / in der ...

Is he/she/it in the ...? –
Yes, he/she/it is. / No, he/she/it isn't.
Ist er/sie/es im / in der ...? – Ja. / Nein.

 ## Let's have lunch   Lasst uns Mittag essen

bread   Brot
cheese   Käse
chicken and chips   Hühnchen mit Pommes frites

cucumber   Gurke

fish and chips   Fisch mit
Pommes frites

ham   Schinken

hamburger   Hamburger

hot dog   Hotdog

ketchup   Ketchup

lettuce   Kopfsalat

lunch   Mittagessen

mustard   Senf

pizza   Pizza

salad   Salat

sandwich   Sandwich

sausage with mashed potatoes
Würstchen mit Kartoffelbrei

soup   Suppe

spaghetti   Spaghetti

tomato   Tomate

cup   Tasse

fork   Gabel

glass   Glas

knife – knives   Messer –
Messer (Plural)

plate   Teller

spoon   Löffel

Can I help you? – I'd like ..., please.
Kann ich dir/euch/Ihnen helfen? –
Ich hätte gerne ..., bitte.

Would you like something to drink? –
I'd like a glass of ..., please.
Hättest du / Hätten Sie gerne etwas
zu trinken? – Ich hätte gerne ein Glas ...,
bitte.

That's ... pounds. – Here you are.
Das macht ... Pfund. – Hier, bitte.

 Hobbies and sports
Hobbys und Sportarten

basketball   Basketball

book   Buch

(to) do   tun, machen

fun   Spaß

great   großartig

hobby – hobbies   Hobby – Hobbys

ice skating   Schlittschuhfahren

interview   Interview

(to) love   sehr gerne mögen, lieben

okay   in Ordnung, OK

(to) play football   Fußball spielen

(to) play the piano/the guitar
Klavier/Gitarre spielen

(to) read   lesen

reporter   Reporter

(to) ride a horse   ein Pferd reiten

(to) ride a bike
Fahrrad fahren

(to) run   rennen, laufen

snowboarding   Snowboarden

sports   Sport(arten)

sports star   Sportstar

(to) swim   schwimmen

tennis   Tennis

What's your hobby? – My hobby is ... /
I like ...   Was ist dein Hobby? –
Mein Hobby ist ... / Ich mag gerne ...

Do you like ...? – Yes, I do. /
No, I don't.   Magst du ...? – Ja. / Nein.

Can you play ...? – Yes, I can. /
No, I can't.   Kannst du ... spielen? –
Ja. / Nein.

My day Mein Tagesablauf

morning Morgen, Vormittag
afternoon Nachmittag
evening Abend
night Nacht

at the same time zur selben Zeit
breakfast Frühstück
(to) brush bürsten
(to) call rufen, anrufen
dinner Abendessen
(to) get up aufstehen
(to) go to bed zu Bett gehen
(to) go to school zur Schule gehen
(to) learn lernen
lunch Mittagessen
(to) play spielen
time Zeit
(to) watch TV fernsehen

What do you do at … o'clock?
Was machst du (normalerweise)
um … Uhr?

I do my homework. Ich mache
Hausaufgaben.

 Shopping Einkaufen

apple Apfel
biscuit Keks
cheese Käse
chocolate Schokolade
chocolate bar Schokoriegel
egg Ei
ham Schinken
honey Honig
ice cream Eis(krem)
lemonade Limonade

lollipop Lutscher
milk Milch
orange Orange
orange juice Orangensaft
spinach Spinat

book shop Buchladen
cart Einkaufswagen
cash register Kasse
clothes shop Kleiderladen
computer shop Computerladen
music shop Musikgeschäft
price tag Preisschild
products Produkte, Erzeugnisse
restaurant Restaurant
shelf – shelves Regalbrett – Regal
shoe shop Schuhgeschäft
shop assistant Verkäufer
shop Geschäft, Laden
shopping bag Einkaufstasche
shopping centre Einkaufszentrum
shopping list Einkaufsliste
sports shop Sportgeschäft
supermarket Supermarkt
sweets shop Süßwarenladen
toy shop Spielwarenladen
(to) try on anprobieren

Have you got … on your shopping list?
Hast du … auf deiner Einkaufsliste?

In the supermarket (book shop …)
I can buy … Im Supermarkt
(Buchladen …) kann ich … kaufen.

Excuse me, please. Where can
I buy …? – Go to … It's on the … floor.
Entschuldigen Sie, bitte.
Wo kann ich … kaufen? – Gehe /
Gehen Sie zu … Das ist im … Stock.

 ## Jack and the beanstalk
Jack und die Bohnenranke

apple pie   Apfelkuchen

beanstalk   Bohnenranke

blood   Blut

castle   Schloss, Burg

(to) climb (up/down)   (hinauf/hinab) klettern

Englishman   Engländer

fairy tale   Märchen

giant   Riese

(to) grow   wachsen

(to) live   leben

magic bean · Zauberbohne

new   neu

(to) sell   verkaufen

(to) smell   riechen

Yummy!   Lecker!

 ## Transport   Verkehrsmittel

boarding pass   Bordkarte

car   Auto

clockmaker   Uhrmacher

detective   Detektiv

(double-decker) bus (Doppeldecker-)Bus

(to) drive   fahren

famous   berühmt

ferry   Fähre

left-hand traffic   Linksverkehr

map   Landkarte, Stadtplan

museum   Museum

old – oldest   alt – älteste(r, s)

plane   Flugzeug

station   Bahnhof, U-Bahn Station / U-Bahn Haltestelle

taxi   Taxi

thief   Dieb

train   Zug

underground   U-Bahn

How can I get from … to …?
Wie kann ich von … nach … gelangen?

You can take the …
Du kannst / Sie können den (die, das) … nehmen.

Let's take the …
Lass(t) uns den (die, das) … nehmen.

I'm sorry!   Es tut mir leid!

 ## Wild animals   Wildtiere

big   groß

(to) bite   beißen

clever   schlau

(to) climb   klettern

dangerous   gefährlich

elephant   Elefant

fast   schnell

fat   dick, fett

funny   komisch, lustig

giraffe   Giraffe

hippo   Nilpferd

jungle   Dschungel

lion   Löwe

long   lang

monkey   Affe

(to) run   rennen, laufen

snake   Schlange

strong   stark

tail   Schwanz

tall   groß, hoch

tortoise   (Land-)Schildkröte

trunk   Rüssel

wings   Flügel

zebra   Zebra

zoo   Zoo

(to) chew   kauen

lake   See

(to) pull   ziehen

rope   Seil, Strick

tug-of-war   Tauziehen

Guess my animal: It's … /
It has got … / It can … / It lives in …
Errate mein Tier: Es ist … /
Es hat … / Es kann … /
Es lebt in/im …

At the doctor's   Beim Arzt

back   Rücken

backache   Rückenschmerzen

(to) bleed   bluten

(to) breathe   atmen

(to) bump   anstoßen

(to) burn   sich verbrennen

(to) cool   kühlen

ear   Ohr

earache   Ohrenschmerzen

head   Kopf

headache   Kopfschmerzen

neck   Nacken

neckache   Nackenschmerzen

(to) pinch   zusammendrücken

(to) vomit   sich übergeben

My ear (neck …) hurts.
Mein Ohr (Nacken …) tut weh.

I've got an earache (a neckache …).
Ich habe Ohrenschmerzen
(Nackenschmerzen …).

I'm sick.   Ich bin krank.

Next, please.   Der Nächste, bitte.

What's the matter (with you)?
Was fehlt dir/Ihnen?

Your leg (arm …) is broken.
Dein/Ihr Bein (Arm …) ist gebrochen.

Cool it.   Kühle es.

Get your medicine.
Hole deine Medizin.

Get a plaster or a bandage.
Hole ein Pflaster oder einen Verband.

Put pressure on the wound.
Übe Druck auf die Wunde aus.

Call 112.   Rufe 112 an.

Going to Scotland
Nach Schottland reisen

castle   Schloss, Burg

(to) discuss   besprechen

(to) go fishing   zum Angeln gehen

Highland Games   Highland Games

hill   Hügel

lake   (der) See

Loch Ness   Loch Ness

map   Landkarte, Stadtplan

mountain   Berg

Nessie   Nessie
(to) plan a trip   eine Reise planen
river   Fluss
Scotland   Schottland
sea   Meer, (die) See
(to) take a photo   ein Foto machen
(to) wait   warten

I/We want to go to …   Ich möchte /
Wir möchten nach … fahren.

I'd/We'd like to see …
Ich würde / Wir würden gerne …
sehen.

There's a … / There are …
Dort gibt es (ein, eine, einen) …

On Friday (Saturday …) we go to …
Am Freitag (Samstag …) fahren wir
nach …

On Friday (Saturday …) we visit …
Am Freitag (Samstag …) besichtigen
wir …

 Jobs   Berufe

boss   Chef
bottle   Flasche
busy   beschäftigt
(to) do   tun, machen
(to) do my homework
meine Hausaufgaben machen
doctor   Arzt, Doktor
(to) feed the cat   die Katze füttern
hairdresser   Friseur
(to) help in the house/kitchen/…
im Haus / in der Küche / … helfen

job   Beruf, Aufgabe
(to) make my bed
mein Bett machen
policewoman   Polizistin
room   Zimmer
shop assistant   Verkäufer(in)
teacher   Lehrer(in)
(to) tidy my room
mein Zimmer aufräumen
(to) turn   drehen
(to) walk the dog
den Hund ausführen
(to) work   arbeiten

What do you want to be? –
I want to be a …
Was möchtest du werden? –
Ich möchte … werden.

What are your jobs?
Welche Aufgaben hast du?

How many in your group have
to help in the garden (kitchen …)?
Wie viele aus deiner Gruppe
müssen im Garten (in der Küche …)
helfen?

I have to …   Ich muss …

Meeting people
Menschen begegnen

different   verschieden, anders
friend   Freund, Freundin
funny   komisch, lustig
rainbow   Regenbogen
special   besonders

strength   Stärke
weakness   Schwäche

England   England
English   englisch
France   Frankreich
French   französisch
German   deutsch
Germany   Deutschland
Greece   Griechenland
Greek   griechisch
Italian   italienisch
Italy   Italien
language   Sprache
Russia   Russland
Russian   russisch
same   gleich
Spain   Spanien
Spanish   spanisch
Turkey   Türkei
Turkish   türkisch
world   Welt

Where are you from? – I'm from
England (Germany ...).
Woher kommst du? – Ich komme aus
England (Deutschland ...).

Are you from ...?
Kommst du aus ...?

Do you speak English (German ...)?
Sprichst du Englisch (Deutsch ...)?

Which languages do you speak? –
I speak ...
Welche Sprachen sprichst du? –
Ich spreche ...

 Guy Fawkes   Guy Fawkes

bonfire   Lagerfeuer, Freudenfeuer
fireworks   Feuerwerk
Guy Fawkes Day   Jahrestag der
Guy-Fawkes-Verschwörung,
5. November

 Thanksgiving Day
Erntedankfest

apple   Apfel
bean   Bohne
carrot   Karotte, Möhre
corn(cob)   Mais(kolben)
fruit   Obst, Frucht
Indian   Indianer, indianisch
pear   Birne
pie   Kuchen
plum   Pflaume
potato – potatoes
Kartoffel – Kartoffeln
pumpkin   Kürbis
ship   Schiff
Thanksgiving Day   Erntedankfest
Thanksgiving dinner
Erntedank-Essen
tomato – tomatoes
Tomate – Tomaten
turkey   Truthahn
vegetables   Gemüse

It's Thanksgiving Day.
Es ist Erntedankfest.

I'm thankful for ...
Ich bin dankbar für ...

 ## Christmas in Australia
Weihnachten in Australien

first   erste(r, s)
second   zweite(r, s)
third   dritte(r, s)
fourth   vierte(r, s)
fifth   fünfte(r, s)

Aborigine   australischer Ureinwohner
capital   Hauptstadt
city   Stadt
cockatoo   Kakadu
coral   Koralle
crocodile   Krokodil
didgeridoo   Didgeridoo
kangaroo   Känguru
koala   Koala
kookaburra   Kookaburra
(to) pull   ziehen
reindeer   Rentier(e)

road train   Lastwagen
rock   Fels
sleigh   Schlitten

Merry Christmas!
Frohe Weihnachten!

 ## Easter   Ostern

(to) break   zerbrechen
cardboard   Tonpapier, Pappe
daffodil   Narzisse, Osterglocke
Easter bunny   Osterhase
egg   Ei
eggshell   Eierschale
fireside   Kamin
flower   Blume
hill   Hügel
mountain   Berg

Happy Easter!   Frohe Ostern!